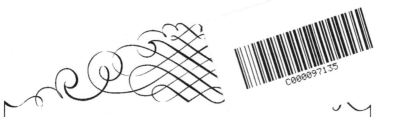

ISBN 978-1-5278-3198-8
PIBN 10892900

1 MONTH OF
FREE
READING

at

www.ForgottenBooks.com

By purchasing this book you are
eligible for one month membership to
ForgottenBooks.com, giving you
unlimited access to our entire
collection of over 700,000 titles via
our web site and mobile apps.

To claim your free month visit:

www.forgottenbooks.com/free892900

English
Français
Deutsche
Italiano
Español
Português

www.forgottenbooks.com

Mythology Photography **Fiction**
Fishing Christianity **Art** Cooking
Essays Buddhism Freemasonry
Medicine **Biology** Music **Ancient
Egypt** Evolution Carpentry Physics
Dance Geology **Mathematics** Fitness
Shakespeare **Folklore** Yoga Marketing
Confidence Immortality Biographies
Poetry **Psychology** Witchcraft
Electronics Chemistry History **Law**
Accounting **Philosophy** Anthropology
Alchemy Drama Quantum Mechanics
Atheism Sexual Health **Ancient History**
Entrepreneurship Languages Sport
Paleontology Needlework Islam
Metaphysics Investment Archaeology
Parenting Statistics Criminology
Motivational

Technical and Bibliographic Notes / Notes 1

The Institute has attempted to obtain the best original copy available for filming. Features of this copy which may be bibliographically unique, which may alter any of the images in the reproduction, or which may significantly change the usual method of filming are checked below.

L'Insti
été p
plaire
ograp
ou qu
de no

☐ Coloured covers /
Couverture de couleur

☐ Covers damaged /
Couverture endommagée

☐ Covers restored and/or laminated /
Couverture restaurée et/ou pelliculée

☐ Cover title missing / Le titre de couverture manque

☐ Coloured maps / Cartes géographiques en couleur

☐ Coloured ink (i.e. other than blue or black) /
Encre de couleur (i.e. autre que bleue ou noire)

☐ Coloured plates and/or illustrations /
Planches et/ou illustrations en couleur

☐ Bound with other material /
Relié avec d'autres documents

☐ Only edition available /
Seule édition disponible

☐ Tight binding may cause shadows or distortion along interior margin / La reliure serrée peut causer de l'ombre ou de la distorsion le long de la marge intérieure.

☐ Blank leaves added during restorations may appear within the text. Whenever possible, these have been omitted from filming / Il se peut que certaines pages blanches ajoutées lors d'une restauration apparaissent dans le texte, mais, lorsque cela était possible, ces pages n'ont pas été filmées.

☐ Additional comments /
Commentaires supplémentaires:

☐
☐
☐
☑
☐
☑
☐
☐
☐
☐

1   2   3

1

2

3

MICROCOPY RESOLUTION TEST CHART

(ANSI and ISO TEST CHART No. 2)

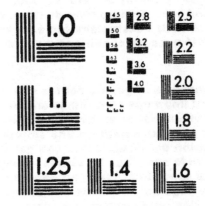

APPLIED IMAGE Inc

1653 East Main Street
Rochester, New York   14609   USA
(716) 482 - 0300 - Phone
(716) 288 - 5989 - Fax

THE STORY OF RIVER

GOLD

AND ITS

RECOVERY

The Demand for Gold—Origin of River Gold—British Columbia's Wealth in River Gold—The World's Gold Production—Methods Employed in Recovering Gold—Reminiscences of the Gold Fields.

By EDWARD BAGLEY.

"There has been a fascination and romance attending the search of the precious metals, and time intensifies rather than diminishes the feeling. Under the magic influences of gold and silver discoveries a spirit of enterprise has been engendered that has brought about the accomplishments of results as unexpected as they were grand and wonderful. The wilderness is peopled, states are founded, and almost an empire established where the presence of civilized man was unknown but a few yeas ago."

Published by

The Business Development Company, Limited

528 Birks Building   **Vancouver B. C.**

Financial agents for the River Gold Recovery Company. Limited ((non-personal liability). Vancouver.

Edward Bagley, Consulting Engineer

Superintendent of the River Goll Recovery
Company, Limited (non-personal liability)
Vancouver.

La   Superintendent of the Thornton Goll
Mining Company, Victoria. Australia

The Story of River Gold

"Gold!"

What a world of romance is attached to the word.

From the earliest times gold has been esteemed the most valuable of all the metals. It is not only distinguished for its rareness, but it possesses many very valuable properties not common to the other metals. It is especially valued for its richness of color, and the fact that its brightness is not liable to tarnish.

The story of gold is one of the most wonderful stories in the world. Millions upon millions, billions of dollars have been extracted from the older gold fields of the world, and today, in our own province of British Columbia virgin fields, of perhaps unparalleled extent await the advent of modern machinery and methods which elsewhere are employed with such marvellous success. Indeed, it may be said that we have here in our rivers a practically inexhaustible reservoir of the precious metal which only requires to be tapped to create a new and flourishing industry giving employment to hundreds of men, peopling the wilderness and making fortunes with a rapidity never surpassed in this or any other country.

The Nature of Gold.

Gold in the pure state is very soft, like lead, and may be easily scratched by the nail. It is more malleable and ductile than any other metal, and is capable of being beaten out into leaves 1/250,000 of an inch in thickness, while one grain of it can be drawn out into a wire 167 yards long.

It is quite probable that gold was the earliest metal to be worked, on account of the fact that the ores of gold are usually less refractory than are the ores of other metals and that it is easily worked into ornaments or coins merely by hammering.

We read in Job 28-1, that "gold is refined," and modern investigations tend to prove that the Ophir of Biblical reference is the southern portion of Metabeleland or the Rhodesia of present fame among mining regions. It is possible and quite probable that the great quantities of gold used in the building and furnishing of King Solomon's Temple came from the vicinity of the present city of Johanneshurg.

Demand for Gold.

At the present time there is a great and increasing demand for gold and other gold-producing countries such as South Africa. Australia and New Zealand are being crowded more and more to increase the empire's supply. The increase in the world's wealth and commerce during the last half-century has created an immense demand for the precious metal — a demand which is bound to increase with the march of science, invention and industrial progress, all of which are factors in adding to the prosperity of all nations and the consequent demand for coinage.

Mining for Gold.

There may be said to be two different and distinct kinds of mining for gold—quartz or lode mining and "placer" or alluvial mining, which consists in the recovery of fine gold deposits in the beds and bars of rivers. With quartz mining this little book has nothing to do, but I shall endeavor to make plain a few facts relating to "placer" mining, explaining the origin of the gold and the various methods employed in recovering it.

The Origin of River Gold.

In alluvial or "placer" mining natural agencies such as frost, rain, etc., have, in the course of centuries, performed the arduous tasks of breaking up the matrix which held the gold, and washing away much of the valueless material, leaving the gold concentrated into a limited area by reason of its great specific gravity. As water has been the chief agent in distributing the gold and gravel constituting alluvial diggings or placers, the banks and beds of running streams in the neighborhood of auriferous veins, are likely spots for the prospector, who finds in the flowing water of the stream the means of separating the heavy grains of gold from the much finer particles of rock, sand and mud. Often the brook is made to yield the gold it transports by the simple expedient of placing in it obstacles which will arrest the gold without obstructing the lighter matter. Jason's golden fleece was probably a sheepskin which had been pegged down in the current of the Phasis till a quantity of gold grains had become entangled among the wool. To this day the same practice is followed with ox-hides in Brazil, and with sheepskins in Ladakh, Savoy and Hungary. This may be deemed the simplest form of alluvial or placer mining.

British Columbia's Wealth in River Gold.

It is officially stated that the gold-bearing gravels of the Quesnel division of the Cariboo districts is 2,500,000,000 to 3,000,000,000 cubic yards, containing $300,000,000 worth of gold. If that be so, there is not less than $1,000,000,000 of gold in the placer deposits of the province. Think what it would mean to commerce and industry in this Province could this enormous amount of gold be recovered. While this is unlikely, and perhaps impossible, there is no reason to doubt but that with the introduction of the improved methods of placer mining employed so successfully elsewhere that many millions can be extracted and a large industry established.

The World's Gold Production.

Mr. Alexander Sharp, the well-known Vancouver Mining Engineer, in a recent address before the Board of Trade in this city, said:—

"The world's gold production in the last quarter of a century equals that of the preceding 400 years. The gold money of the world has doubled in the last twenty years.

The total world production of gold from the discovery of America to the present time is, according to compilation, $16,500,000,000 in coining value. The gold money in 1896 aggregated $4,144,000,000, and in 1916 totalled $8,258,000,000.

"The chief gold-producing countries of the world are (1915) South Africa, $207,000,000; United States, $101,000,000; Australia, $50,000,000; Russia, $29,000,00; and Canada, $19,000,000. It will be noticed that Canada takes fifth place among the gold producing nations of the world, which is very creditable considering the lateness in which railway transportation was employed in this country.

"Six million, three hundred and forty-six thousand and seventy dollars of this gold value was produced from alluvial deposits of Klondike and British Columbia."

Methods Employed.

In the early days of gold-recovery in British Columbia, as in Australia and California, where rich alluvial deposits were common at the surface, the most simple appliances sufficed, and indeed, in this Province, upwards of seventy million dollars worth of gold has been recovered from our rivers chiefly through the use of the pan and rocker, appliances which I am about to describe. Even at the time of writing, scores of individual miners, chiefly Indians and Chinamen, are making good wages along the Fraser, North Thompson and other rivers "panning" or "rocking" out the gold, and the wealth of the sands will be appreciated when it is understood that by these methods only about a cubic yard of "dirt" can be handled daily. A cubic yard is the equivalent of about one and one-quarter tons.

Since the days of '49 the rocker and pan have been chiefly employed by individual miners to extract the gold from the sand and gravel. This is the hardest kind of work, especially for men and youths not accustomed to it; where the pan alone is used to wash out the gold the constant stooping is especially severe on the back.

However, the rocker saved the miners' hands

and by forcing him to keep in use several different sets of muscles enabled him to work without much physical discomfort.

In the shallow workings the individual miner's working equipment consisted of pick and shovel, pan, cradle or rocker and the sluice. A miner's "pan" is about twelve inches in diameter at the bottom. It is of iron and looks for all the world just like a common dairy pan. Sometimes the miner would use his pan for frying flapjacks, and it cannot be denied that it was handy for that purpose, but the practice was frowned on by many miners because of the grease employed in the process. Any grease in a gold pan makes it difficult to retain the fine gold.

When the pan has been filled with gravel or whatever soil was in the bedrock, it would be taken to a convenient pool, stream or even tub, and dipped into the water in such a manner as to take up sufficient water to sluice off the heavier material. This was then thrown out. The process was repeated until nothing remained in the pan except a little fine sand sparkling with particles of gold. This was carefully dried in an iron vessel and the sand blown away, leaving the pure gold.

This, however, was slow and laborious work so the "rocker" was resorted to. The rocker resembles a child's cradle. About six inches from the top is a hopper with a bottom of perforated iron. Earth and gravel are shovelled into the hopper by one man who pours a flood of water into the machine to assist in breaking up the lumps of soil and wash it clear of the gold. The cradle is then rocked backwards and forwards until the gold content of the hopper falls through into a sloping tray below on which are cross bars, called riffles, to arrest the gold.

Before long these methods were found to be too primitive, and the more enterprising miners took to building sluice boxes. In some cases these were merely a single trough, 10 to 12-inches deep, fifteen to twenty wide and twelve feet long. However, as each trough tapered towards its lower end, any number could be easily fitted one into the other and thus forming a sluice thousands of feet in length.

The bottom of the trough was well provided with riffles, sometimes covered with mercury to catch the finer particles of gold. After weeks of sluicing the "clean up" would come. The gold would be carefully collected from behind the riffles; that which had been caught by the mercury would be carefully scraped off. The amalgam formed by the mercury and gold was then squeezed in chamois leather or unbleached calico, which rid it of most of the liquid mercury and retained the solid amalgam. This was then put into a retort and subjected to great heat until all the mercury had been vaporized and conducted through tubes to a condenser where it had resumed its liquid form. This gold was porous and spongy and had to be melted down and run into bars for disposal.

Dredging Methods.

In working auriferous river-beds, dredges have been used with considerable success in certain parts of New Zealand and on the pacific slope in America. The dredges used in California are almost exclusively of the endless-chain bucket or steam shovel pattern. Some dredges have a capacity, under favorable conditions, of over 2,000 cubic yards of gravel daily. The gravel is excavated as in the ordinary form of endless-chain bucket dredge and dumped into the steel sluice leading to the large revolving screen, the finer materials passing on to sluice boxes provided with riffles, supplied with mercury. There are belt conveyors for discharging the gravel and tailings at the end of the vessel remote from the buckets. The water necessary to the process is pumped from the river, as much as 2,000 gallons per minute being used on the larger dredges.

Testing the Ground.

Whenever deposits of a broad area, with considerable and uniform depth, are thought to be valuable, it has become a practice to prove their value by shallow shaft sinking and "prospect drilling." This is a mechanical method and one form of apparatus employed is of the churn-drill type common throughout oil and coal regions. With these portable machines, holes are put down to bed-rock at intervals across the ground. As they are sunk, the holes are cased with iron pipes, the drillings are carefully saved and washed, and the values are estimated for each foot of descent. From the summation and averages obtained from all the holes, a very fair knowledge of the ground's worth can be obtained. This is the method I employed in Australia and which I purpose using in this country, as it eliminates risk and uncertainty and enables the plant to be located where the greatest values are.

Low Cost of Placering.

Arthur J. Hoskin, of the American Institute of Mining Engineers, states in his book "The Business of Mining": "All costs of placering are reckoned per cubic yard washed. Costs have been rapidly dropping during the past decade until now some companies, with extensive operations, are handling dirt at not to exceed three cents per cubic yard for excavating, washing, wasting the refuse, maintenance, repairs, labor, taxes, interest on investment, and the depreciation of equipment." I may say that in Australia costs are kept down to about this figure, for otherwise it would not pay to operate on account of the fact that the rich areas have long been exploited. A company with which I was associated estimated that they could make a handsome profit on sands containing values of only six cents a cubic yard. This being the case it will readily be seen what a large margin of profit awaits a company employing the same modern, intensive methods, as actual tests have proven the existence in this province of large areas, embracing perhaps scores of miles with values ranging upwards from fifty cents per cubic yard.

British Columbia's Fine Gold Problem Solved.

As a boy starting work I began on the fine flaky gold problem, and have made a careful study of it all my life; now I am introducing to this country a machine which I claim will overcome all the difficulties hitherto met in the recovery of fine gold from the river beds of this province. This machine, which is the product of thirty years' experiment, was introduced into New South Wales by Mr. William Roberts, a well-known mining engineer, to whom Australia is indebted for many valuable inventions. It was tested in Sydney in the presence of many experts and adopted by the New South Wales government and put in their Clyde Works at Strathfield (where I first saw the machine) to test alluvial sands for the miners.

I arranged with Mr. Roberts to form a small company in Victoria and test the machine over there. A pair of them were built in Melbourne under the supervision of Mr. Roberts and put to work on a stack of tailings containing fine, flaky gold. We took out of this stack of 36,000 cubic yards 690 ounces of gold worth $20 per ounce, and when it is remembered that each machine will handle twenty cubic yards of river gravel and sands per hour the wonderful possibilities of the process will be recognized. The machine separates the gold and a concentrator, working in conjunction with it, saves the black sands which have considerable value as they are used by the steel companies in their blast furnaces, and for other purposes.

Substantial improvements have been made on Mr. Roberts' invention and fresh patents applied for, embracing Canada and America, where extensive and practically virgin areas of golden sands exist.

This new gold recovery process will, in my opinion, revolutionize the recovery of river gold, or "placer" mining in these countries and will be used on bucket dredges, cableway excavator systems with travelling towers, with

12

steam shovels on bench areas, side by side with portable plants of unique design, similar to that which I erected and worked in Victoria with 100-ton capacity per hour. Small outfits also will be made for miners which will have twenty times the capacity of "Rockers" and can be worked by hand.

Among the many valuable additions to the mining industry which came from Australia is the now famous "oil flotation process" which has meant millions in dividends from copper mines in British Columbia and America. In my judgment, this fine gold saving process has even a larger range and cannot fail to introduce a new era in mining, building up a huge gold producing, wage paying, money making industry of the greatest benefit to this and other communities.

The machine has been cabled for from Australia and shortly will be set up in Vancouver. A fifty-ton heap of gold-bearing gravel will be brought from the Fraser River, and a test or demonstration given in the presence of mining engineers, practical miners, representatives of the Chamber of Mines and the Boards of Trade in different cities of the Province, representatives of the press and the public generally. The idea is to thoroughly test the gravel for gold and other minerals before it goes into the machine and then to test the tailings afterwards. If no gold or minerals are found in the tailings the efficacy of the machine will have been demonstrated and conclusive proof furnished that British Columbia's fine gold, platinum and black sand problem is finally solved.

Mining the Greatest Industry.

It is common to hear the assertion made that "More money is put into the ground than is taken out of it." This is epigrammatic, but inexact. What actually goes into the ground is not money but work. For the moment we pass by the hundreds of individual fortunes that have been made in mining, and which range from scores of thousands to scores of millions, and will consider only the average results. The comparison with other industries will excite surprise.

The United States census of 1900 collected some very complete information about the number of persons and amount of capital engaged in our national industries and the value of their output. The census inquiry was very minute and exhaustive. An analysis of the returns is interesting and instructive. Briefly summarized they are as follows:

8,285,616 persons were engaged in Agriculture. The total value of farm products shows that the amount produced per capita was.. $297.00

521,806 were engaged in Forest industries (logging, sawmills, and the like). The net value of the product per man engaged was............ 425.00

4,476,884 were engaged in the manufacturing industries. Deducting the cost of materials and miscellaneous expenses, the net value of products per man was................... 765.00

84,439 were employed in Mining, Milling and Smelting of gold, silver, copper, lead and zinc (coal and iron not included here.) The value of the output for each man employed was 1,910.00

Average returns per man engaged:—

    $297.00 in Agriculture.

    $425.00 in Forest Industries.

    $765.00 in Manufacturing.

    $1,910.00 in Metal Mines.

In the census year the mines of the metals named returned on an average to each of their workers six and a half times as much as the farms, four and a half times as much as the forests, and two and a half times as much as the manufacturers.

This was the average return, in spite of the numerous amount of unproductive labor thrown away in ill-advised mining ventures; while the workers in other fields had all the advantages of labor-saving machinery, and of the highly developed manufacturing economics which key up every man's production to the highest possible pitch.

The National Banker has said: "Statistics show the combined dividends paid by the gold and silver mining companies of the United States are greater than the combined dividends paid by all of the banking institutions of the country."

Bradstreet's and Dun's commercial agencies supply the somewhat startling addenda that but 36 per cent. of all legitimate mining investments fail, as against 54 per cent. in commercial lines.

U. S. Government figures show the following returns on capital invested: Railroads, 3 per cent.; national banks, 6¼ per cent.; insurance 11 per cent.; lumbering, 14 per cent.; manufacturing, 14 per cent.; MINING, 182 per cent.

There is one thought that will always comfort any person who is engaged in furthering legitimate mining: Wealth acquired from a mine is not wrested from any being but Mother Earth, and is not, therefore, in the class with the much discussed 'tainted money" that is said to be wrung from unfortunate human beings.

While the business of gold recovery is yet in its infancy in this country, and the rich placer areas contain the wealth which they have guarded almost since the beginning of time, there is reason to believe that the introduction of modern methods will revolutionize the industry and make it one of the most important and beneficial in the province.

Reminiscences of the Australian Gold Fields.

While now an enthusiast regarding Canada, having made up my mind to settle down in this country and use my knowledge and experience as best I can to develop its wonderful resources in minerals, a few reminiscences of the old days in Australia may prove of some little interest to the reader, as I am confident that before long in our own Province of British Columbia we shall see the public take as keen and hearty a concern in legitimate mining as do the people of the Antipodes.

I was born in the year 1864 at Hepburn, near Daylesford, Victoria, which is situated at the South Eastern extremity of the mainland of the Commonwealth of Australia. My birthplace was famous in the early fifties for its gold production, and is today a favorite resort for summer visitors who not only slake their thirst from the pure, clear effervescent mineral water which flows down among the rocks, but also take a great deal of pleasure in viewing the big mines which still operate on the quartz lodes at Daylesford.

Here I lived until six years of age and well remember my father taking me down to the big Chinese camp near the old race course and showing me where, years before, he had worked a rich claim. He told me how he found their sluice boxes being robbed occasionally at night and how he and his partner kept watch one night and found four Chinamen at the boxes at 2 a.m. Their method was to lift some of the riffles off the sluice, put the contents in bags, then throw in sand and gravel and let the water through to cover their depredations. As they were leaving, father and his mate rushed the party and both being powerful men they soon made short work of the Chinese, notwithstanding the fact that they put up a stout fight with their heavy bamboo sticks. One of the Chinamen pretended to be dead and the rest fled. The supposed dead man was carried to father's camp and when put down on the ground there was not a move in him until they applied soap suds to his eyes and started to cut off his pigtail. Then "John" let out a thunderous yell, followed by a shout like a stunning thunder-clap "Wha' for?" The small diggers camp of whites was soon aroused and a messenger sent to the police camp. Not a bit too soon, either, for the camp was soon surrounded by about two hundred Chinese, armed with long bamboo poles, who came to rescue their mate. The whites kept their quarry, and the rest of the excited crowd of Orientals, at bay with pistols and iron bars until the police arrived to disperse the crowd and take charge of the captive.

The Gold Rush of '51·

At an early age we removed from Hepburn to Fryer's Creek, some twenty miles distant, where father was manager of the "New Era" quartz mine, with a forty head battery and ten tribute claims. Long before my time "Golden Gully" on the site of which our house was situated, was the scene of a great gold rush in 1851. However, by the time our family reached Golden Gully, the rich alluvial surface ground had been worked out, sustaining a few fossickers only, although around the Fryer's Creek district big quartz mines were at work and considerable gold being won. I remember that after every rainstorm, myself and other boys would go "specking" and in the washed out gutters could always find some good sized colors from a grain to a dwt.

We remained in this district until I was eleven years of age, when our family removed to Taradale, about ten miles distant. Here my father secured the right on a royalty basis to treat all the slums and tailings from one of the big alluvial mines of the district, the "Ironstone Hill," managed by Mr. Tom Symonds.

Saving Fine Gold.

Here tests showed that considerable fine, flaky gold was being lost by the company, going away in the sludge from the steam puddlers and over the sluice boxes. My brother William, a year older than myself, and I, assisted my father for four years on this mine, saving the fine gold until the company adopted similar devices, and we had to quit. As I was then about sixteen years of age, I got work in the mine trucking at one dollar and a quarter per day, and worked there for another year. About a year later I obtained a position at the "Confluence" mine, Malmsbury, about a mile

further away, as a striker in the blacksmith
smith shop, and there learned to sharpen the
drills and other tools used. In spare time I
had to assist in cutting mine timbers and help
on the steam puddling machines and sluices.
Afterwards I got a position underground as
mate to James Taylor, the shift boss, where I
learned all the difficult work of timbering in
heavy running drifts, the use of breastboards,
and so forth. I often think of the old manager, McMaster, an efficient and careful man,
and how he used to stand at the boiler door as
we came up from below at 8 a.m., and ask the
thirty or forty men "Did you do your set last
night?" "Yes, sir, yes, sir," was the invar-
iable reply, as every faceman was supposed to
do his set a shift, that is to say, to put in his
false set of timber, drive home the laths, put
his main set and breastboards in. It was hard
work for the facemen and his mate to do this,
and the wage was only seven shillings a day.
About this time a terrible misfortune happened
our family: my father was in Gippsland, Victoria, and when inspecting a quartz mine for
a Melbourne Company, walking along a drive
examining the rock, he stepped into an uncov-
ered winze which connected with a deeper
level, and was killed.

Gold Rush in New South Wales

Passing over the next few years which I
spent buffeting with the world in the attempt
to assist, as best I could, my widowed mother,
gaining a miscellaneous and valuable experience in the school of hard knocks. I will come
to the year 1887, thirty years ago, when a big
gold rush set in in the west of New South
Wales, known as the Peak Hill rush. I immed-
iately repaired to this field, taking with me a
monied partner, Mr. Janezek, and commenced
staking lease applications wherever likely looking ore was found outcropping. Rough shanties
doing duty as stores, skittle alleys, billiard
rooms, boxing saloons and all kinds of busi-
nesses quickly sprung into existence and many
thousands of men, comprising every descrip-

tion of person clad in every variety of attire,
with their provisions and camp requisites carried in all sorts of odd vehicles, were soon upon
the scene of the gold discovery. A prospector
sunk a shaft about two miles away from the
Peak Hill and bottomed on rich alluvial gold.
This news reaching Sydney fanned the spark
into a flame and as there was a big maritime
strike on at the time, a general rush set in and
soon 16,000 men were on the field. They came
in coaches, drags and wagons from Dubbo, No-
long and other railway stations, and soon there
was a canvas town miles in length—a striking
scene by night, with crowded hotels, street
vendors shouting their wares, drunken liggers,
free fights, thousands of camp fires, loud hand-
clapping and shouting at various entertain-
ments and hundreds of moving lanterns as the
diggers threaded their way among the tree
stumps in uncleared streets. It was a gay
and extraordinary scene. Robberies were rife,
and a murder was committed during my stay
there. However, the field did not prove to
be the bonanza anticipated; the golden hole
proved a pot-hole only, and the majority of the
quartz lode outside the Peak Hill Proprietary
being not rich enough to pay, the rush soon
ended in a fizzle.

Some time after this I went investigating
mining properties in the New England district
in Northern New South Wales, five hundred
miles from Sydney, and at a place called Fair-
field I took an option over "Barkers United"
mine, which I floated in Sydney, later secur-
ing an option over the "Nil Desperandum"
mine at the same place, which I floated in Woo-
woomba, Queensland. Here I was appointed
General Superintendent and remained for a
year or more, until the Mareeba rush broke out
in North Queensland. This field I visited, but
it was a quartz field, and while the surface out-
crops showed some rich specimen stone, all
the ground had been staked, and the owners
were not disposed to sell, save at prohibitive
prices. Then I went further inland and investigated many quartz properties, also up the

Russell and Mulgrave Rivers from Cairns and away to the back of Cooktown.

Charters' Towers.

After spending several months in the Cairns and Cooktown district I left for Townsville, where I took train to Charter's Towers, about 100 miles inland. This field has long been famous for its great gold production, the reefs there being worked for over 5,000 feet in depth. I found it a big and prosperous city on tableland country with little or no timber in sight. I remained here for some weeks investigating the chances on this field and studying the laws which govern in the deposition of quartz lodes in this granite field, so unlike the corrugated strata of Bendigo, Victoria, with the anticlinal and synclinal folds in the slate beds. There I found that the mines that were worth having were not available, and that the available mines were not worth having, so I proceeded further down the Queensland Coast to Rockhampton to visit Mount Morgan, twenty-five miles further inland. This was a thriving township of some 7,000 inhabitants. I went through this big mine which is world renowned for its production of mineral wealth, being even today a big dividend payer, and could fill pages with interesting matter relating to its early history, the struggles in getting the first plant over the Razorback, the geological features of the place, the theories advanced relating to the impregnation of the Kaolin dykes by means of silicious solutions from deep subterranean passages permeating the porous rocks for many hundreds of feet around the main pipe of overflow thus forming a rich cone going deep down in the earth—rich in gold and copper.

Looking For a Second Mount Morgan.

Mr. Meinburg was the first manager of this mine, and together we spent months travelling within a radius of one hundred miles looking for a second Mount Morgan, which, he was firmly persuaded, existed. We had a good

camping outfit, a four-wheeled horse-drawn
vehicle and all the necessary tools, but, although we travelled a long way, and came
across some prospectors who showed us some
small gold-bearing veins, we did not succeed
in finding anything rich.

Shortly after our trip, Meinburg died, and a
few of his friends, myself among them, erected
a monument in the shape of a shaft built up
with quartz stones with a windlass on top.

I stayed five years in this district and in
conjunction with Mr. V. M. Dowling, then
general manager of Mount Morgan, inspected
many new discoveries in the districts which
were from time to time reported. Subsequent-
ly I was appointed General Mine Superintendent of a group of gold and copper mines known
as the "Morinish" and the "Phoenix- Alli-
ance" thirty-six miles from Rockhampton
and about twenty-five miles across the country
from Mount Morgan. I occupied this position
for four years, then resigning to return to my
native state, Victoria.

River Dredging in Victoria.

Leaving Queensland some time later I spent
fifteen more years in Victoria. River dredging
was booming at the time and in this industry
I spent nearly twelve years. Bucket dredging, pump hydraulic dredges, jet elevator
sluicing were all the rage around Castlemaine,
on the Loddon River, the Ovens and Buckland
Rivers and elsewhere, and the improved port
running pump invented by Kershaw and Dav-
ies of Castlemaine caused the formation of
hundreds of companies to exploit the old
diggings. As some of the pump dredges were
paying dividends in this district on as low as
100-ozs. to the acre the system was generally
adopted all over the state, and in the running
streams bucket dredges being employed. On all
the diggings once famous for their gold values
there was a wild rush staking the ground and
some thousands of miles of gold runs were sur-
veyed off and floated into companies.

I then was appointed mine manager and engineer for the "Galatia Gold Mining Company" at Malmsury, where I had spent many years in my teens. At this mine I erected a winding and crushing plant.

Later I resigned and was appointed engineer for the "Great Posiedon Alluvial Gold Mining Company," at Tarnagulla. A big rush had set in on the Posiedon field. Big lumps of gold weighing many pounds in weight were picked out of the shallow ground. Later I saw the models of these nuggets in the Geological museum in Melbourne. They would cover a table about 6-feet by 4-feet. The "Posiedon" nugget gross weight was 953 ounces. This ranked as the fourteenth largest nugget found in Victoria and was found twenty inches below the surface in the year 1907.

The World's Largest Nuggets

The largest nugget found in Victoria was the "Welcome Stranger" which weighed in the gross 2,520 ozs. (250 lbs. weight) and the lucky finders, Messrs. Deason and Dates, were advanced $50,000 by the London Chartered Bank at Dunolly. This nugget was found in a cart rut on February 5th, 1869. The second largest nugget was found at Bakery Hill, near Ballarat, its value being $46,600. And so on down Victoria has produced a succession of nuggets which outrival all known records. But the largest mass of gold that the world has ever seen was discovered at Bevor and Holtermann's claim at Lill end in the Hillgrove district, New South Wales. Its height was 4-feet 9-in., its width 2-feet 2-in., and its thickness 4-in. As quartz was mixed with it it had to be broken up, but $65,000 was offered for it and refused.

A miner in West Australia "dollied" out $73,000 worth of gold in 1890 from the cap of a reef on the Yalgoo field and $97,000 worth was won in a few days by the discoverer of the "Wealth of Nations" mine. Space forbids my giving a list of the twenty-seven largest nuggets found in Victoria or the extensive notes which I have compiled on the origin of

22

nuggets in alluvial as well as in quartz lodes.

The rush to the Posiedon field led investors to stake in the deep lead areas; bores put down across the Loddon River showed the ancient watercourse to be 200-feet deep and as the watershed from the Posiedon field would be a tributary lead to the main channel companies were formed and big alluvial mining plants erected.

The Freezing Process Adopted.

The erection of the plant of the Great Posiedon mine took me about one-half year, but as the main shaft could not penetrate the heavy running drift below 80-feet on account of the boiling up of the sand inside the heavy steel sinking box, the collapse of the shaft threatened. I advised the Board of Directors to adopt the freezing process and submitted a report describing the method as employed in France and Belgium. The directors adopted the idea and the shaft was sunk and bottomed in ice without a break through. Enormous sums have been lost in Victoria trying to pierce heavy running drift—losses which could have been avoided by the use of this highly successful process.

I have now had about forty years practical experience in mining in quartz, in fine gold, gold and copper ores; have erected nearly all classes of mining plants, including Huntingdon Mills, Krupp Ball Mills, Stamper Batteries, Alluvial Steam Puddling Plants; have sunk deep alluvial shafts in drift and familiarized myself with every method of deep alluvial workings in running drifts, including the various blocking and pannelling systems employed.

Since coming to British Columbia I have investigated many miles of river gold areas and satisfied myself as to their extent and richness. To my mind there is no country in the world presenting such a wonderful opportunity for the introduction of the modern, intensive methods which elsewhere have met with such great success.

During my career I have frequently been

asked whether I consider investments in mining propositions safe and profitable. In reply to this prevalent question I cannot do better than to quote the words of the late Cecil Rhodes, the millionaire owner of mines in South Africa, who, in a speech several months before he died said: "I speak advisedly and say what every man who has investigated knows to be the truth, that less money is lost proportionately in mining and investment stocks than in any business or investment on earth. A good mining stock will pay the investor more easily 20, 30, 40, 50 and 100 per cent. annually than municipal bonds, railroad bonds and stocks or government bonds can possibly pay 5 per cent. The proper time to buy mining stock is when the company is first offering its stock to the public, thus getting the benefit of all future advances."

Technical Press, Ltd., Vancouver, B. C.

CPSIA information can be obtained
at www.ICGtesting.com
Printed in the USA
BVOW06s1126090118
504830BV00026B/357/P